Words to Say

David Gwilym Anthony

Illustrations by
Merfyn C Davies

Copyright © David Gwilym Anthony 2002

All rights reserved

No part of this publication may be reproduced, stored in a retrieval system, or transmitted in any form or by any means, without the prior permission in writing of the publisher.

First published in Great Britain 2002
by Pen Press Publishers Ltd
39-41, North Road
Islington
London N7 9DP

ISBN 1-904018-43-2

Printed and bound in Great Britain by
Creative Print and Design

A catalogue record of this book is available
from the British Library

Illustrations by Merfyn C Davies
Cover Design by Jacqueline Abromeit

CONTENTS

Preface
Acknowledgements
Foreword by Helena Nelson

Roots
2 A Winter's Tale
3 Bloodlines
4 One-Way Ticket

People
7 Over America
8 To Gerard Manley Hopkins
10 Tambourine Man
11 For The Beatles
12 Who'll Hold Their Hands?
14 Heilige Nacht
15 Look Away
16 Flower Seller

Family Matters
20 Boy Soldier
22 For My Daughter
23 On a Photograph of a Young Child
24 Words to Say

Perspectives
28 Water Bearer
29 Tanka
30 Crossing the Border
31 Knowing the Score

Travelling
34 Father of the Man
35 Navigator
36 The Road Taken
38 Running on Empty

Departures
40 On the Suicide of a Friend
41 A Small Mystery on Gray's Field
42 I Thought You Were a Friend
43 On Seeing a Photograph of Marie Watson
44 Remembered Wings
46 Out of the Night
47 Nearer to Thee

Seasons
50 Hawthorn
51 I Saw a Snowdrop
52 After a Snowfall
54 Tallyman
55 Plague

It's Not What You Say
58 Triolette
59 Stuffing It In
60 Rep's Rondeaubout
61 My Bulkhead Light

Chestnut Puree
64 Cushioning the Blow
65 Family Troubles
66 To Die For
67 Bearing the News
68 Who's Afraid?
69 Entomologist
70 Under the Weather

71 Notes
72 About the Author

Preface

The explosion in internet use has created a new world of opportunity for writers everywhere, and there are thousands of internet workshops where we can share our work and experience.

It's been said there are more people writing poetry nowadays than reading it. Perhaps there always were; or possibly contemporary poetry is becoming too arcane and internally focused for the general reader. If so we must try to change.

I correspond with a number of poets through the internet, among them my formalist friends at Sonnet Central (HYPERLINK "http://www.sonnets.org/" http://www.sonnets.org/) and Eratosphere (HYPERLINK "http://www.ablemuse.com/erato/Ultimate.cgi" http://www.ablemuse.com/erato/Ultimate.cgi). I'm very grateful for their help and advice.

Special thanks to Helena Nelson for her careful reading and invaluable suggestions.

ACKNOWLEDGEMENTS

Some of my poems have appeared in the following books and magazines:

UK
Acumen
Candelabrum
Poetry Scotland
The Sonnet at the Millennium (Anthology)
Worm

USA
Artemis
Avatar Review
Carnelian
Light Quarterly
Pierian Springs
Susquehanna Quarterly
The New Formalist
Writers' Hood

JAPAN
Contemporary Ten Thousand Leaves Anthology (Gendai Manyo Shu)
Eisuke Shiiki's Ran Pan Un
Tanka Journal

Foreword

I first met David Anthony in the 'cyber sea' he speaks of in his poem Navigator. Initially through online workshop discussion and later through email contact, I came to know him virtually. Virtual? The etymology of the word relates to virtue and also to essence: the essential quality of a person or thing. Some – and I am among their number – would suggest that this virtual route is as true a way of knowing a person as any other, and truer than many. I learned very quickly, for example, that David was a painstaking craftsman, with an informed love of poetic method, someone who could not only turn his hand to a sonnet with the ease born of loving practice, but also that rarer being – someone who could breathe life into it. His delight in the craft was immediately obvious, as was his instinct for lyric line and elegiac phrase. In his ready response to life events, he struck me as wise and kind, careful and true.

David's poems are rarely mere ornaments: they contain real thought, often difficult thought at that. He is an honourable disciple in a long tradition, using the sonnet, for example, to introduce a question or problem, before offering his own considered resolution. His thought is compressed, personal and satisfying. Penetrating in his insights, he avoids didacticism. His utterance is characterised by interrogatives, perhapses, and a tone of conjecture. At the same time, he is playful with words, form and intent. Sometimes it is a very serious playfulness; at other times, it is unashamedly mischievous.

The humorous poems in this collection are no less carefully made than their serious counterparts. They bubble up from an irrepressible sense of fun. Who could resist Cushioning the Blow or Who's Afraid? Such pieces serve to persuade that poetry can both begin and end in delight.

But this writer is a nature poet too; often the natural world is the focus for recurring themes of change and loss. However, although an elegiac tone recurs, often with haunting plangency ('Why are you weeping, May Tree, May Tree?') the sense of affirmation overrides any feeling of absolute loss. It may be partly the formal grace of the lines which leaves me with a sense of something positive, even in a stark piece like Who'll Hold Their Hands?, but I think it's more than that. This is a poet who accepts both dark and light, pain and joy, but maintains steady faith in the human spirit. In contemplating some of the worst tragedy we have known in recent years, he can marshal words of lyrical simplicity to affirm a solid truth:

> 'A man spoke out for the human race
> on his pocket telephone.'

Faced with sadnesses both small and large, David Anthony's poems, with disarming modesty and memorable grace, really do find 'the proper words to say'. Read them, and you will see.

Helena Nelson
July 2002

ROOTS

A Winter's Tale

A cry cut through the winter's wind. 'Who died?'
the student asked, his focus far away
from college friends who'd just arrived to stay.
'Poor Hywel Jones,' his grandmother replied.

The guests had read of spirits that abide
in Celtic lands – those keening ghosts who stray
when souls are crossing – and they felt the fey
forebodings carried where the cold wind cried.

Across the road a carpenter once more
bent to his task. The same old man who made
cots for the village babies, now must build
a thing to hold no hope. His power saw
began to turn again. The cutting blade
bewailed an ending, and its wild cry chilled.

Bloodlines

They're pictured wearing baubles carved from bone,
woad-daubed and fur-clad, flaunting tribal scars.
Such disrespect – such crude depiction – mars
the memories embedded in the stone
and in my blood, my every chromosome.
Why paint their culture worthless next to ours,
those men who traced the movement of the stars
and built Stonehenge before the birth of Rome?

Their mysteries live on within each cairn
and megalith, though little else remains:
like us they learned what pride and progress cost.
If we could call their spirits to return,
would they stand silent, awed by all our gains –
or stricken, seeing everything we've lost?

One-Way Ticket

They closed the line and just the track remains.
The miners' railway where we used to play
in far-off summers when I came to stay,
echoes with the ghosts of long-gone trains.

Cwm Cynfal and the Ceunant ring with wild
remembered songs of childhood. Years away
mean nothing there. When I returned today
they called me as they once had called the child.

The rest is altered irretrievably.
My kin died years ago or else moved on –
no point in staying, once the work was gone –
and local people don't remember me.

My ties are broken far beyond repair.
The line is closed and just the tracks are there.

PEOPLE

Over America
(Jeremy Glick, United Airlines Flight 93, 11 Sept. 2001)

A man spoke out from a lonely place
on his pocket telephone.
As he heard what end he would have to face
a man spoke out from a lonely place.
To bow to force could be no disgrace
yet he vowed to fight for his own.
A man spoke out for the human race
on his pocket telephone.

To Gerard Manley Hopkins

Your spirit hovered quivering, poised on air
of sense and sound, charged like a lightning rod:
now flashing out to seize the grace of God,
now plummeting in darkness and despair –
despair! Did wisdom really bring you there,
where tired generations trod and trod,
where feet convey no feeling, iron-shod,
where hopelessness hangs heavy everywhere?

Sometimes I wonder, did you understand,
without the dark your candle could not glow?
Your soul was tortured by self-reprimand,
self-crucified, self-loathing; yet I know
the God you loved and hated took your hand
at last, and led you safe where no storms blow.

Tambourine Man

His hair a thicket, voice a rasping saw
cutting through cant and conscience's decay –
my scruffy hero channelled youth's dismay
and changed the world in 1964.
His music called to me: I heard with awe
wild songs – they wheeled and soared above the day
then, swooping, drove indifference away.
Glad to be young, I stood at heaven's door.

He calls again, and how could I resist
a ragged clown behind a reverie
still chasing wraiths within the day's grey mist?
It's darker now: I cannot sense or see
a way ahead, but I can dance. Hey! Mist-
-er Tambourine Man, play a song for me.

(for Bob Dylan's 60th birthday, 24 May 2001)

For The Beatles

You showed us all, we all need love,
and love is all. We need
your compass, or we fear to move.
You showed us all, we all need love,
and how those simple songs can prove
abiding friends indeed –
you showed us all. We all need love,
and love is all we need.

Who'll Hold Their Hands?
(on the murder of Jamie Bulger)

Sometimes an image strikes a shocking blow.
I've seen deceit, concealed beneath fake care,
cut like a whip and strip the senses bare.
A bitter man's betraying kiss was so;
or two unruly boys on video –
ignored by passers-by (not their affair) –
who held a toddler's hand and led him where
there are dark truths we do not choose to know.

'Hanging's too good!' 'They don't deserve to live!'
(But whose is the betrayal we recall?)
Did Christ, the friend to thief and fugitive,
greet Judas' kiss with empathy or gall?
They were our sins and so we can't forgive:
just ten years old! May God forgive us all.

Heilige Nacht

A broken tank stands sentinel before
the salient where Rundstedt's soldiers tried
to force a passage as their army died
and Christmas came, in 1944.
Though it was clear they couldn't win the war,
they fought to thrust their enemy aside
– for comrades, or obedience, or pride –
and knew, in failing, they could do no more.

Did the Child, who all those years ago
brought hope at Christmas, look on in despair?
Perhaps, though I believe it wasn't so.
My thoughts return to lonely valleys where
the human spirit suffered in the snow
but still endured. It stood unbroken there.

Look Away
(for Stonewall Jackson)

God-fearing Patriarch, you rose to smite
the North as Samson smote the Philistine:
the South's defender, certain of divine
endorsement, confident your cause was right.
You whipped the Yankees squarely every fight
and championed your people's proud design,
till wanton bullets from the Rebel line
at Chancellorsville, foreshadowed Dixie's night.

Come, tired soldier, let us cross the stream
and rest beneath the shadow of a tree.
The centre fails; intruders reign supreme
and raze your land through Georgia to the sea.
The shadow deepens, darkening a dream
as Dixie bears a cross to Calvary.

Flower Seller

Glimpsed roses at a roadside stall: so bright
a contrast to the city's traffic haze;
rich with the peace and warmth of summer's days
and quiet reveries of dark and light;
seen only for a moment – there, then gone.
Such wistful beauty, such a brave display,
stands out against the drabness of the day,
confirming even here our dreams live on.

But wayside seller, looking at your face,
I see your flowers are only goods to sell
with no innate significance. Ah, well,
there's little value in the commonplace;
and yet I wonder, trapped within life's schemes
and compromises, did you sell your dreams?

FAMILY MATTERS

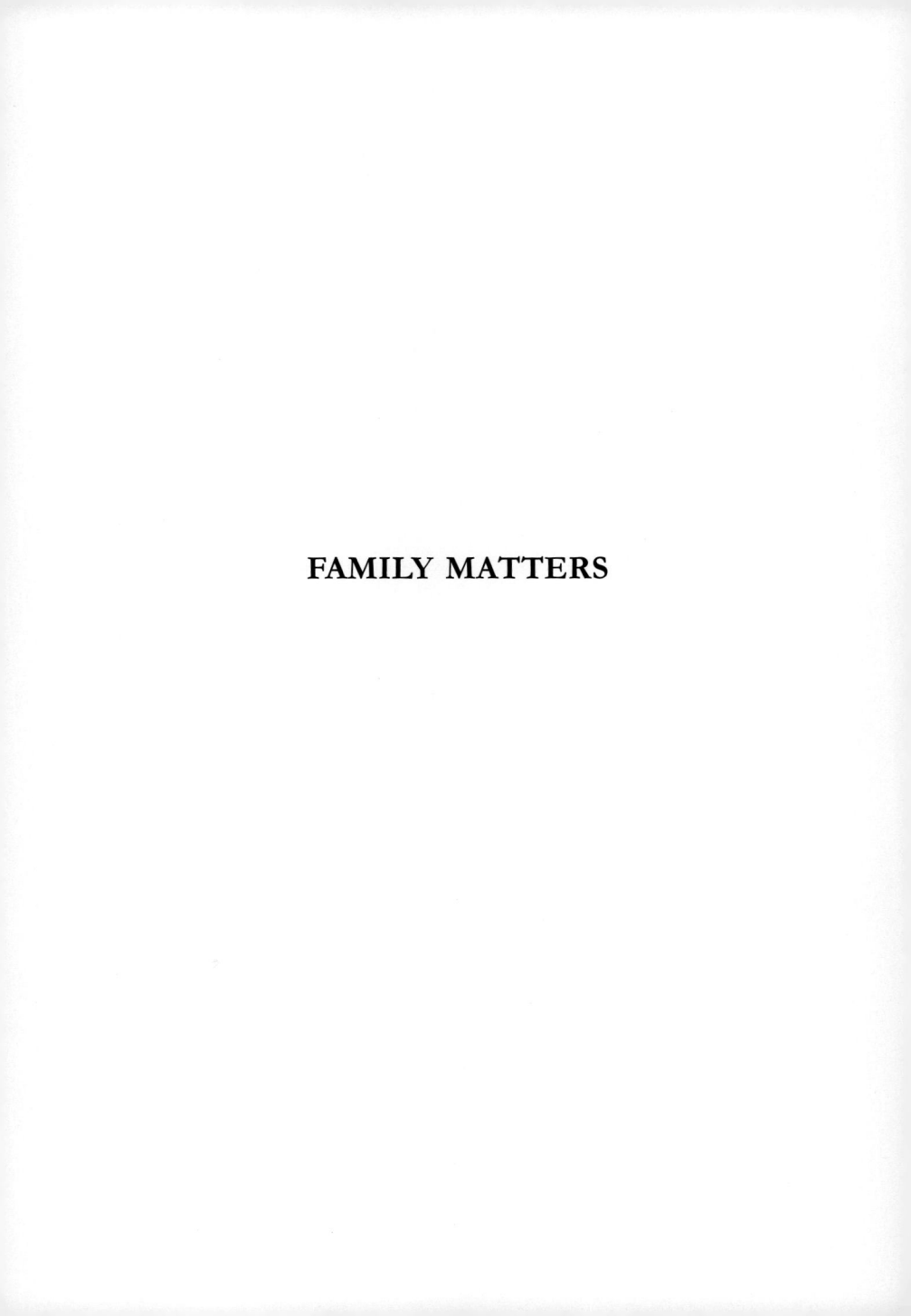

Boy Soldier

He posed for the photographer with pride:
a soldier leaving home whose childish grace
betrayed his fourteen years, although his face
gave little clue to how he felt inside.
I think his mother looked at it and cried –
it caught his spirit. Time could not deface
that image, nor time's challenges displace
his fortitude, till all was swept aside
one vivid day – the day my father died.
Some people say our lives can only be
like marks upon the sand, indifferently
reduced to nothing by the evening tide.
Still, these remain: a quiet memory,
a fading photograph, and part of me.

For My Daughter

It's funny how I never saw you grow.
I seem to miss what's nearest as a rule,
far too preoccupied – a busy fool,
blind to the way the seasons come and go.

What shall I give, since now you're going too
and will be gone a while? Although you're brave
and self-assured, I know I rarely gave
a sign to show how proud I was of you.

I give it now, with love; but love's no gift:
it's yours by right. Because you're going far
I'll give a gentle light to be your star,
and all my hopes to hold when life's adrift.

I'll give them all, though all I have would be
no gift beside the gift you were to me.

On a Photograph of a Young Child

Shining eyes and golden hair,
little soldier standing there –
may the future take you where
stars will always shine at night,
days will all be golden-bright.
May the touch of care be light.

Words to Say

The priest knew all the proper words to say.
He'd never met her, but he had a note.
He mentioned everything her brother wrote,
and said she'd had a good life anyway.

The old piano she would often play
still holds remembered cadences of those
Welsh melodies she loved; but I suppose
we'll sell it now, since Betty's passed away.

I saw her schedules written on a chart
pinned to the study wall: she'd meant to speak
to Mum, and booked the dentist for next week.
Strange, how the little things can break your heart.

I'd watched her growing weaker day by day,
but never found the proper words to say.

PERSPECTIVES

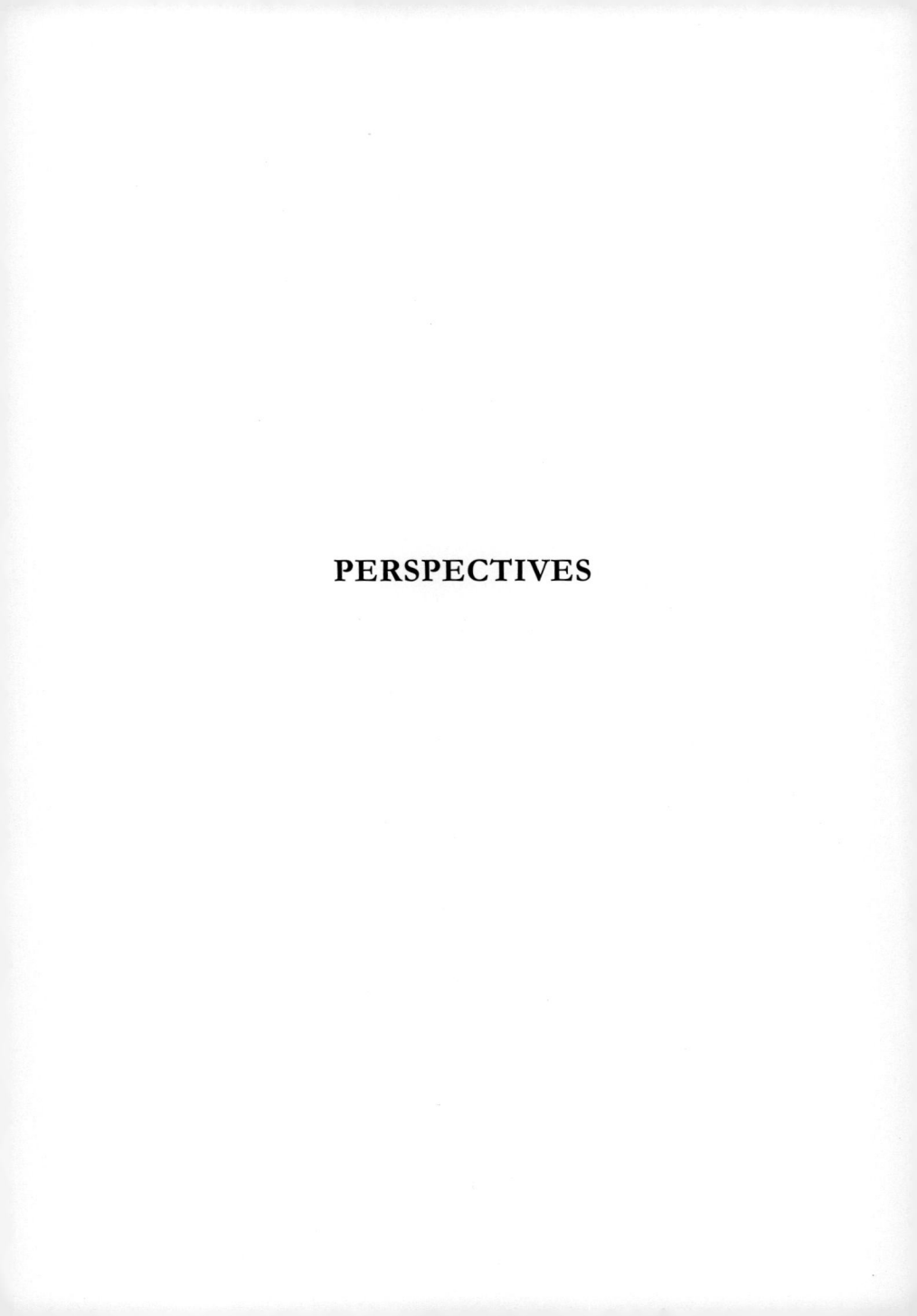

Water Bearer

Each dawn before the sun devoured the shade
and seared the arid land, a potter strode
down to the well along a dusty road
to fill a well-used water jar he'd made.

As he returned one day a stranger said,
'Your jar is fractured. Anyone can see
you waste your time and labour fruitlessly.
The water spills along the track you tread.'

The potter answered, 'Though it leaks, it still
retains enough for me and I would not,
for all its flaws, discard my battered pot.
It has a special purpose to fulfil.'

Where he had passed a radiant display
of flowers danced to greet the breaking day.

Tanka

I, when young,
meant to change the world.
Now I see
how the world has changed
from my point of view.

Crossing the Border

Fences are never needed: Herdwick sheep,
gracing the Lakeland hills with gentle bleating,
have learned the boundaries they are to keep.
Fierce Viking settlers recognised the greeting
of each flock heafted to its native fell,
and cared for them through hardship, knowing well
how troubles pass, and all revives with spring.
A harsher husbandry is now depleting
those ancient herds, and old ways are retreating.
Can thought deny the heart's remembering?
May we return some part of all we take,
and so reclaim the wisdom lost to man
to know our bounds; then nature will remake
a truer borderline than fences can.

Knowing the Score

The slights I cherish sing to me
their old seductive song.
It's friends who always wound the worst –
the list I keep is long.
I don't much like the counterpoint,
a quiet voice, but strong:
'Choose wisely when remembering;
Love keeps no count of wrong.'

(1 Corinthians 13)

TRAVELLING

Father of the Man

Daunted by the shadows in my mind,
uncertain where the hazy pathways led
and frightened by the darkness up ahead,
I saw my Youth approaching from behind,
and paused and waited, thinking what to say.
We'd broken contact many years ago
and hadn't much in common; even so
his certainty might help me find the way.

He turned to me, but coldly, with a frown,
and I fell silent, angered, filled with such
dismay because this parent asked too much,
mixed with regret for having let him down.

So burdened by the weight of wasted days
we drew apart, and went our different ways.

Navigator

The drive engaged; electric sails unfurled,
then filled; I keyed a course – h t t p: –
and started out across a cyber sea
in search of fellow feeling in the world.
I navigated oceans brightly pearled
with scattered islands of affinity,
whose harbours sometimes seemed like home to me,
safe havens when distress and discord swirled.

Seafarers slightly known and swiftly gone,
some here to learn, and all with things to say:
those strangers warming in the light that shone
from empathy, had little time to stay.
Minds met a moment, touched and travelled on
to look for something lost and far away.

The Road Taken

Youth's urgency permitted no delay,
and many paths diverged. I didn't know
which one to take or where I ought to go,
and settled for a broad and trodden way
because it offered light and company;
but as my friends dispersed along the road
I travelled on alone, and often strode
through places I had no desire to be.

At evening everything becomes opaque,
and circumstance has turned the track I chose
back on itself, much nearer now to those
remembered byways I shall never take.
This is a light to me when dark is near:
the paths diverged, but all at last led here.

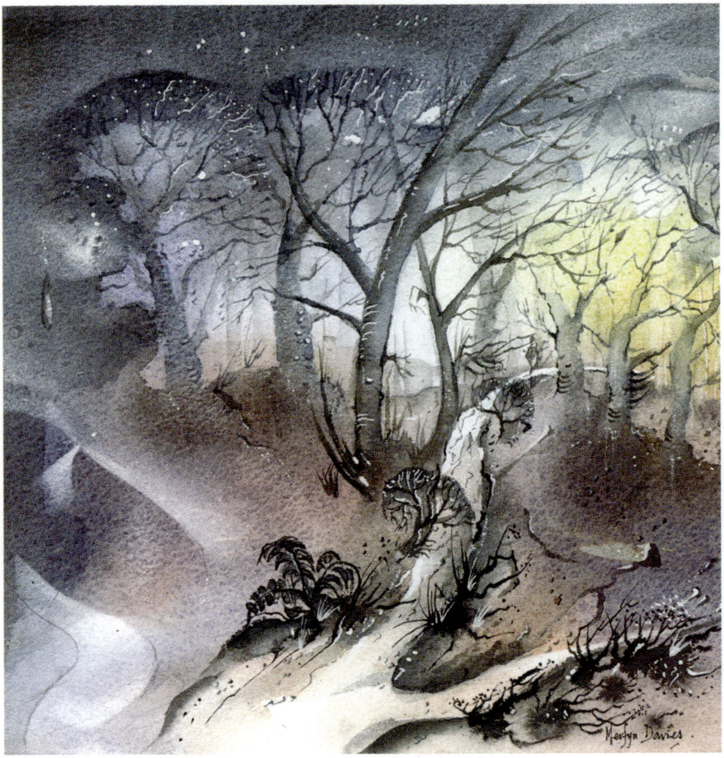
Merfyn Davies

Running on Empty

Preoccupied, I overtook the years,
and never saw the moments racing by.
The future seemed worth chasing then, and I,
knowing how expectations outrun fears,
was restless, restless – unprepared to wait
or turn to where the present was. The pain
of losing things I'd never see again
was nothing; but it troubles me of late.

Time modifies perception. Even though
what does remain is altered, and ahead
are lonely roads where apprehensions spread,
I will not fear to go where shadows grow –
still restless, though anticipation's gone.
The gauge reads empty, but the wheels roll on.

DEPARTURES

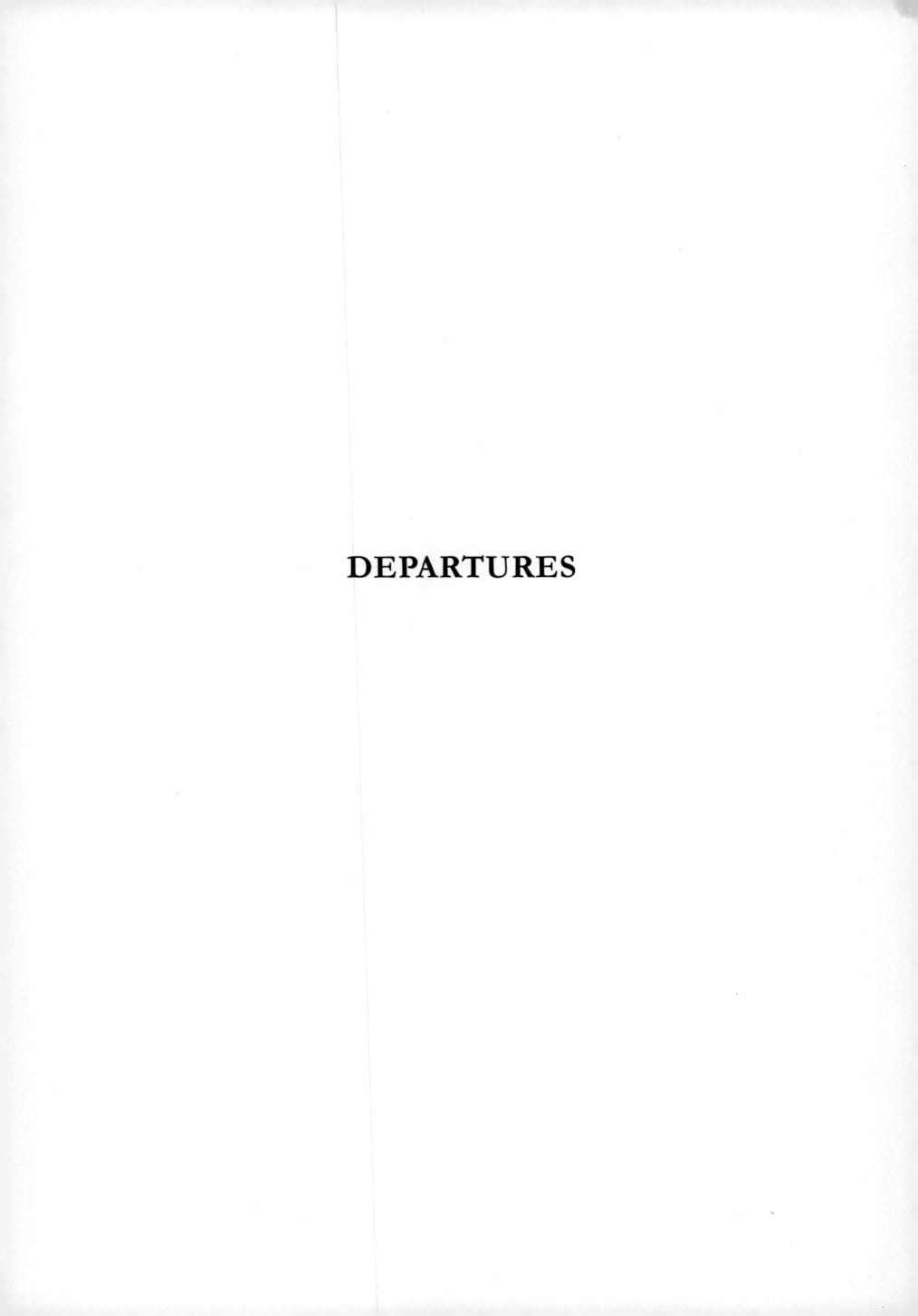

On the Suicide of a Friend

'God help the kids!' I heard the neighbours say —
so quick to judge, though mostly they were kind.
They saw the sorry mess you left behind
and thought you took the coward's selfish way.

The coward's way? No, not that I can see.
Despair's a snare. They say a fox will gnaw
its fettered foot and sacrifice the paw.
What desperation drove you to break free?

Nor were you selfish. Just beneath the calm
the darkness gathered; I have known it too.
It touched those near. It's my conviction you
believed you were protecting them from harm.

God — if there's a God — will grant you rest:
you failed, we all do, but you did your best.

A Small Mystery on Gray's Field

She sat alone and wretched in the cold,
untagged and collarless, abandoned there.
Someone had loved her once – the signs of care
apparent, she was pampered, plump and old.
The neighbours gathered, anxious and involved,
till one of us, because the light was dim,
picked up the dog and brought her home with him.
Not every problem is so simply solved.
The owner had been elderly, I'd say –
and kind, to judge him by his mongrel. Though
time's devastation hardens us, I know
he'd not in life have treated her that way.
When twilight, fading, turned to monochrome,
God held him safe, perhaps, and brought him home.

I Thought You Were a Friend

I knew you well and thought you were a friend,
and yet you gave no sign you meant to go.
Is this the proper way for it to end?

The hardest thing for me to comprehend
was why you failed to say goodbye, although
I knew you well and thought you were a friend,

and never doubted once I could depend
on you. To my regret it was not so.
Is this the proper way – for it to end

so brusquely? I had always meant to spend
more time with you. It was a telling blow
from one I knew, and thought of as a friend.

I would have stood beside you to defend
against the fear, though all I really know
is this: the proper way for it to end

is not the way the passing-bells pretend –
they ring with falsehood, sonorous and slow.
There was no proper way for it to end
for you who left me, though you were a friend.

(*in memory of MM*)

On Seeing a Photograph of Marie Watson

The hurt is deep within a face
transfixed by shock – a bleak grimace
in monochrome. The suffered blow
allows no human comfort, so
her spirit's found another place.

The gravitas is gone, the grace
her age has earned. Can youth debase
what youth becomes, and never know
the hurt is deep?

Harsh are the values we embrace,
and small our lives; how soon our trace
will vanish unremarked, although
we mourn the way the victims go
to meet an end we fear to face.
The hurt is deep.

Remembered Wings

Year after year their timing was the same.
As early summer took the place of spring
my swallows came, and briskly gathering
would breed, then raise their young and so proclaim
hope's renaissance. Each darted sharp as flame
between the earth and sky, remembering
old haunts, despite long miles of wandering.
This year I waited but they never came.

Autumn's a time for leaving: cherished things
are embers, as remembered flames burn low,
and vanish with the chill the first frost brings;
a time to grieve, though now it isn't so:
never to greet those brave arriving wings
spares the paint of parting when they go.

45

Out of the Night
(on the execution of Timothy McVeigh)

We saw your death – they showed it on TV –
and had revenge, if vengeance was our goal.
You thanked the Gods, whatever Gods may be,
and spoke of your unconquerable soul.
We shared a God – no, not the one whose whole
existence was compassionate, who tried
by promising redemption to console
his wayward children, and was crucified.
We chose your sterner Deity as guide,
with ancient tribal precepts, and a sword.
Though hope and charity did not abide,
faith lived when our uncompromising Lord –
not often merciful, but always just –
demanded eye for eye, and dust for dust.

Nearer to Thee

We waited sadly for the news
and felt what was to come:
those children in the photograph
were not returning home.
Small hope was ended with a bleak
announcement on TV,
and in our church the choir sang
"Nearer my God to Thee."

Can God be near when malice lurks
throughout the world He made;
when every generation sees
its innocents betrayed?
Each evil lessens all of us -
who lets such evil be?
But grief fills churches - grief, and shame -
and brings us nearer Thee.

We search for meaning, finding none;
for hope, where hope has died.
Yet there's a message we received
when Christ was crucified:
lives unforeclosed are beacons, bright
however dark the sea.
Take them; take them with their grace,
and hold them near to Thee.

(in memory of Holly and Jessica)

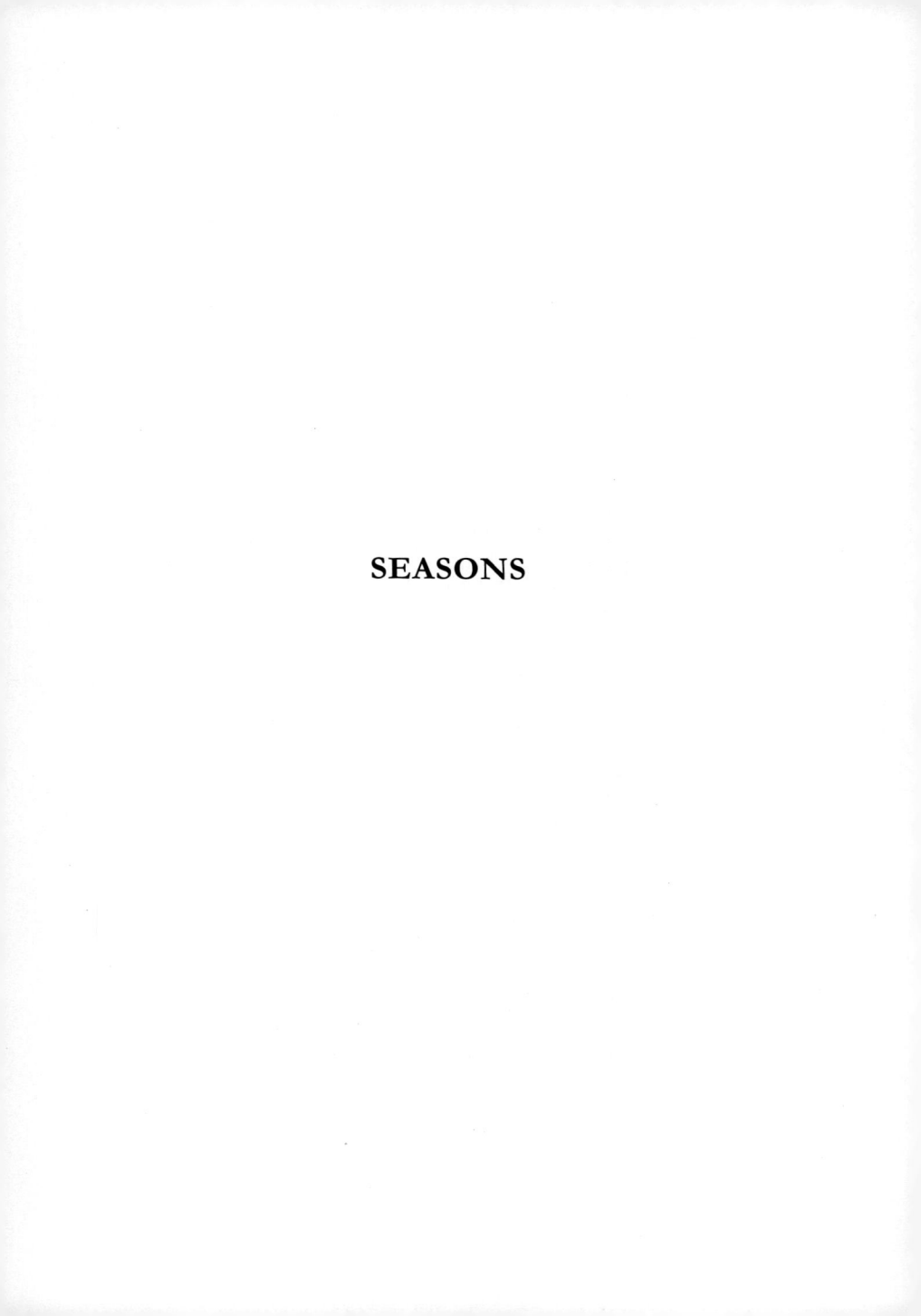

SEASONS

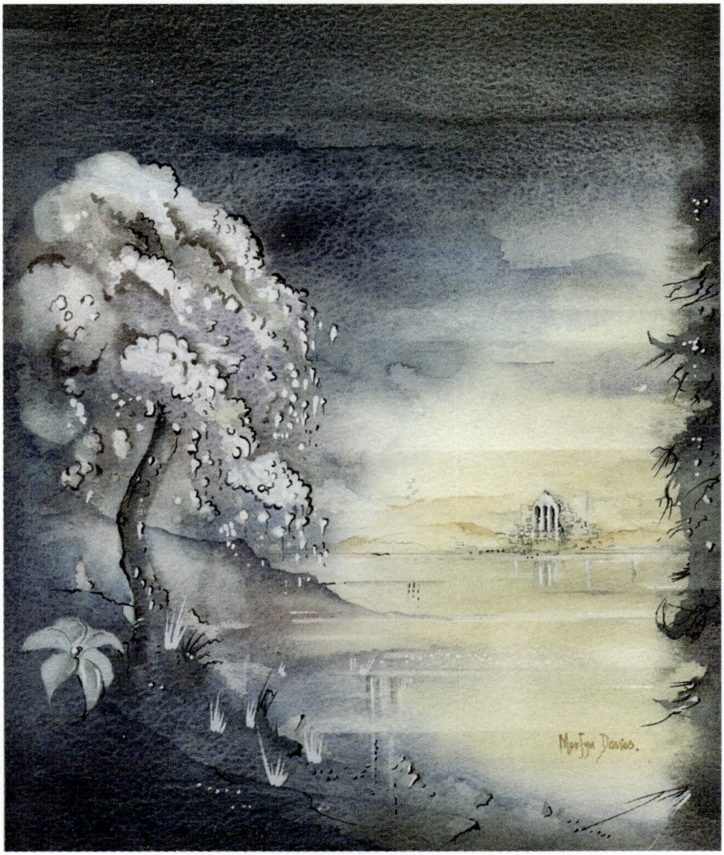

Hawthorn

Why are you weeping, May Tree, May Tree,
why are you weeping, May?
Springtime's fresh and the sun is high;
there is no blue like the morning sky,
and winter's far away.
The season's glad so why be sad?
Why are you weeping, May?

Why are you weeping, May Tree, May Tree,
why are you weeping, May –
shedding your tears of perfect white,
pure as sorrow and white as light,
in garlanded decay?

Is it care for seasons yet to be?
Let's look away and refuse to see:
the year is young and so are we
and winter's far away.
Thoughts so cold never trouble me,
so cease your weeping, May.
Please cease your weeping, May.

I Saw a Snowdrop

I saw a snowdrop yesterday.
Proclaiming spring's around the corner
seems premature; I'll simply say
I saw a snowdrop yesterday.
It filled my head with thoughts so fey
I called my Muse to thus forewarn her:
'I saw a snowdrop yesterday
proclaiming spring's around the corner'.

After a Snowfall

This is a quiet season; nothing mars
the earth's serenity. Above, the night
pays homage to the moon; attendant stars
hold lanterns up to view a world of white.
Beneath the perfect surface, out of sight,
incarcerated in the winter's care,
are poor creations lost without the light,
like secret dreams now withered in despair.
But Nature comforts those imprisoned there
with hope, where all was hopeless and forlorn:
a hint of freshness, and the starting stir
of growth to promise us a world reborn.
In Nature as in man, a quiet face
hides winter's grief and spring's creating grace.

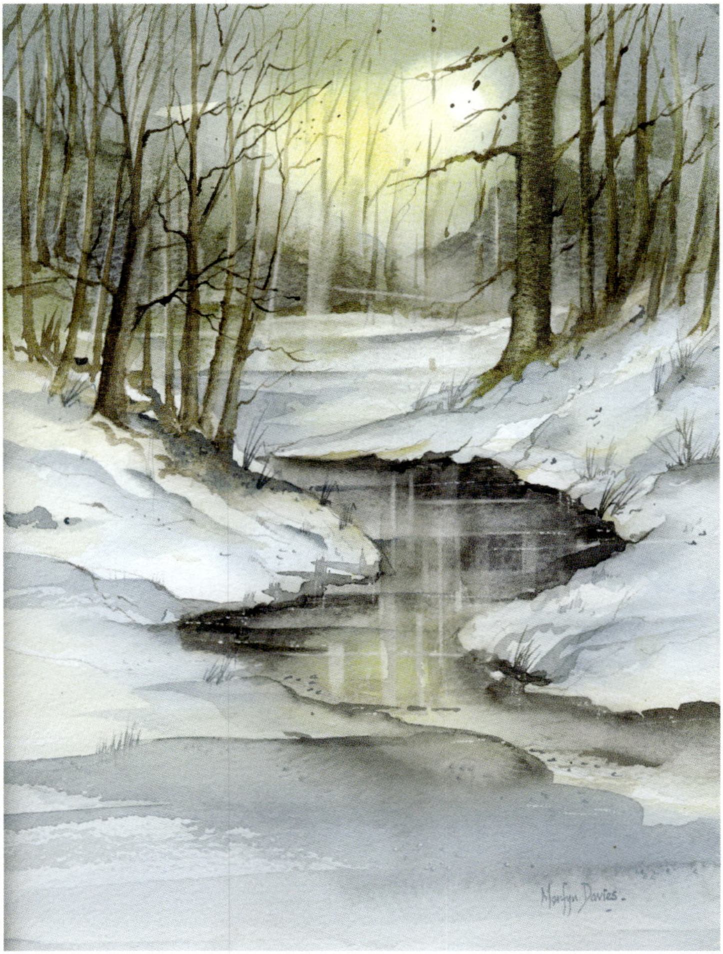
Merfyn Davies

Tallyman

It seems no time since warmth replaced the cold,
and nature's careful plans were first displayed
in buds along the foxglove's stem, arrayed
profusely and preparing to unfold.

Tall tallyman, I know the price you pay!
Your clustered blossoms nodding to the dawn
fade one for every evening, as you mourn
the counted fall of every summer's day.

Too soon a wilder wind arriving scours
the season's bright creations, stripping bare
the hedgerows and the woodland clearings where
you sacrifice your last and lonely flowers –

still beautiful, although the best are past;
and missed the most, because they were the last.

Plague
(On the foot and mouth epidemic, Spring 2001)

The guns are loud across the land tonight.
Grim beacon flames flash out from shire to shire
and horror groans without an end in sight.

Best not to look as marksmen expedite
such slaughter! Hired to empty every byre,
the guns are loud. Across the land tonight

Spring flinches at the foulness of the blight
that lurks within the pall above each pyre
and horror groans without an end, in sight

of pallid flames where all is darkly bright.
So draw the blinds and turn the music higher –
the guns are loud across the land tonight!

Send off the children. Let them still delight
in childish things; don't tell them life's a liar
and horror groans. Without an end in sight

there seems no point. Why carry on, why fight?
Not only cattle perish in the fire,
and horror groans without an end in sight.
The guns are loud across the land tonight.

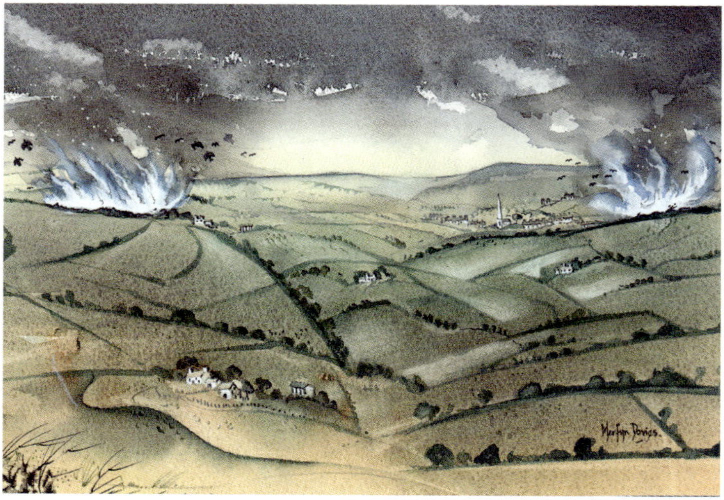

IT'S NOT WHAT YOU SAY

Triolette

I think I'll write a triolet –
but does it rhyme with get or gay?
I'm ignorant I know, and yet
I think I'll write a triolet
and make a rhyme with gay – or get –
Who gives a toss whichever way?
I think I'll write a triolet –
but does it rhyme with get or gay?

Stuffing It In

Today I feel the urge to do a sonnet:
I'll see to it before the morning's out.
Just one word rhymes with sonnet, but no doubt
a slant can be insinuated – Done it!
So far so good. Enjambment helps: let's run it
between the lines. I'm half-inclined to flout
the rule insisting on a turn, about
line nine. Screw Petrarch's horse! Why am I on it?
But like the horse I'm knackered, so let's try
to reach a lazy climax; soon be there:
just ease it in, far better not to force it.
Sonnets are like those garments ladies buy –
I'm thinking of restraining underwear.
Sometimes the bulges overcome the corset.

Rep's Rondeaubout

Traffic jams are so much fun –
better far than boring meetings.
Get the week's expense claim done!
Phone a friend with cheery greetings!
Never worry when you're late –
fast lane life won't take you far.
Some things are in league with fate –
traffic jams are.

(*after Leigh Hunt*)

My Bulkhead Light

My bulkhead light was broken;
I broke it yesterday.
I never meant to break it;
Alas alackaday!

It served me well and truly;
It made the darkness bright.
'Twas hammer-blow that laid it low
And robbed me of my light.

I hied me down to Do It All
And hailed the Overseer:
'Where will I find a bulkhead light?'
'We keep them over here.'

My bulkhead light is mended;
I mended it today.
'Twill never be the same, though;
Alas alackaday!

Come all ye Home Improvements men,
Take heed and learn from me:
A bulkhead light costs seven pounds,
Including V.A.T.

CHESTNUT PUREE

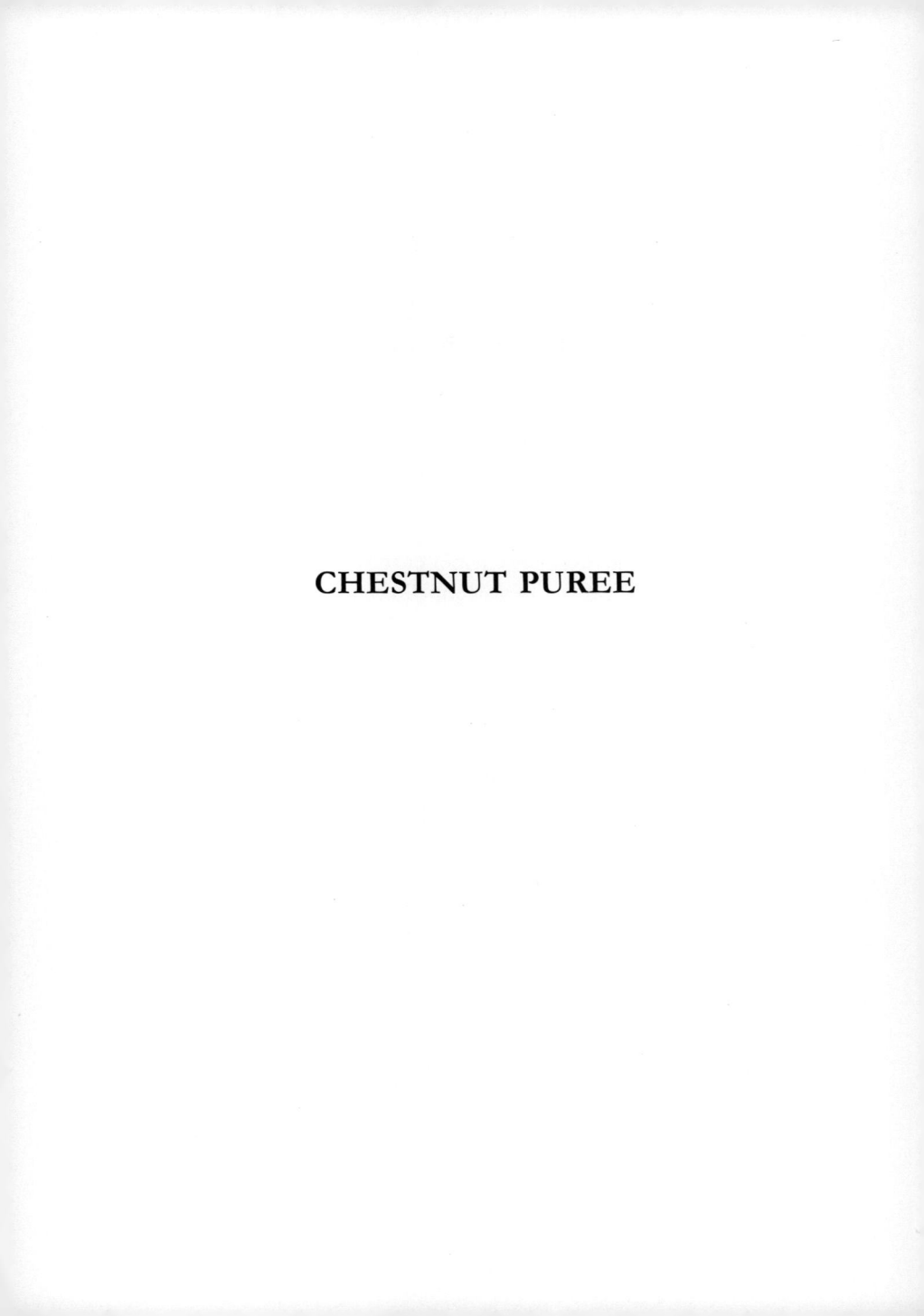

Cushioning the Blow

We thought it best to leave the cat with Ted
along with Grandma, when we went away.
No sooner were we home from holiday
than, bluntly, he announced the cat was dead.

'Listen!' I said, 'Bad news is better told
obliquely - like this: "Bess went climbing on
the roof, and fell. Her legs and back were gone.
They tried to save her but she was too old". '

Ted – who's direct but not a thoughtless man –
was chastened (so he said) and mortified.
'Don't worry, Cousin Edward,' I replied.
'We all drop clangers. By the way, how's Gran?'

'Not great,' he said. 'In fact, to tell the truth,
last night she went out climbing on the roof...'

Family Troubles

We had our problems. John, my younger brother,
was burdened by a speech impediment;
and Father (who'd been wounded when he went
to war) had one leg shorter than the other.

John said to him, while battling with his stutter,
'D-D-D-Dad, I do believe I know
a way to fix your limp. W-when you go
out walking, keep w-one foot in the gutter.'

Dad tried it, and he thought he was in clover.
His limp was cured and he was walking well,
till much to his chagrin he tripped and fell.
A bus was passing by and ran him over.

He said, 'Your stutter can't be fixed, Son, but
it helps if you would keep your big mouth shut.'

To Die For

Aunt Bessie has a talent: when she bakes,
the flavour drives you wild. My cousins say
their father Tim, a regular gourmet,
married her for love – of chocolate cakes.

Poor Uncle Tim was feeling far from well –
in fact, was on his deathbed – when the scent
of baking half-revived him. Off he went
to find the source of that seductive smell.

Each step was painful as he tottered down
to taste the treat. At last his feeble hand
grasped hungrily. Bess slapped it sharply, and
dismissed him with an irritated frown:

'Clear off to bed, and put the buns back too.
I made them for the funeral, not for you.'

Bearing the News

She heard the sound of banging at the door.
'Are you the Widow Murphy?' Jimmy cried.
'They call me Mrs Murphy, that's for sure,
but no, I ain't no widow,' she replied.
Says Jim, 'It may have been a fact before,
but take a look what's on me cart outside.'

Who's Afraid?

Miss Jones, who takes the younger children, prides
herself on spinning yarns: at five years old
the kids, when entertained, are good as gold,
and sometimes say surprising things besides.
They loved the story of the pig that tries
to build a house of straw – the one the bold
and wicked wolf will wreck; a tale best told
with care, explaining what it signifies.

'The pig,' she told them, 'found a turnip bed
made out of straw, and asked if he could dig
a little up. Guess what the farmer said?'
'I know,' cried Jude, one hand above her head,
and standing (since she wasn't very big):
'Well, bugger me – here comes a talking pig!'

Entomologist

Nell shines among the brightest academics
within the world of entomology.
All bugs enthral her, and the bumblebee
inspired her noted *Insectile Polemics*.

The other day I called around to tell her
I'd spotted her VW in town,
going too fast (it nearly ran me down)
and driven by a shifty-looking feller.

'Oh God, he's got my insects!' Helen cried.
She had my sympathy – it takes such care
to build collections – and I wondered where
they'd been: the boot, or on a seat inside?

'No, neither place; I keep the inside clean:
they're on the outside, squashed against the screen.'

(for H B)

Under the Weather

I went to see the doctor since
I wasn't feeling fit.
My head was hurting and my hands
were shaking quite a bit.
He asked me if I drank a lot
(the nosy little git).
I answered, 'No, in fact I spill
the greater part of it.'

NOTES

p. 4 *One-Way Ticket*
"Cwm Cynfal and the Ceunant": the valley and gorge of the River Cynfal, pronounced "Koom Kunval and the Kuynant"

p.12 *Who'll Hold Their Hands?*
Jamie Bulger, aged two, was abducted and murdered in Bootle, Lancashire, by ten-year-old Jon Venables and Robert Thompson in 1993. The boys were released from custody in 2001.
The abduction was captured on a precinct security video, showing Jamie being led away, holding hands.

p.14 *Heilige Nacht*
The German Ardennes offensive (the Battle of the Bulge), December 1944-January 1945, was fought in bitter cold and heavy snowfall and was halted by Allied (principally American) counter-attacks and by fuel shortages.
A German tank still stands beside the road at Celles, marking the furthest point of the advance on Christmas Eve, 1944.

p.15 *Look Away*
General Thomas 'Stonewall' Jackson was shot by accident by his own men following his victory at Chancellorsville in May 1863. Arguably that bullet was the pivot on which the American Civil War turned: Jackson never lost a battle, but after his death the South lost every major battle except Chickamauga.
His last words were: 'Let us cross over the river and rest under the shade of the trees.'

p.30 *Crossing the Border*
Herdwick sheep: a rare breed specific to the hills of Cumbria, with a homing instinct known as 'heafting' or 'heathing' in Cumbrian dialect.
There was mass slaughter of livestock during the foot and mouth epidemic, 2001.

p.43 *On Seeing a Photograph of Marie Watson*
Aged 77, Marie was mugged by a youth for her takeaway supper and died a few days later.

p.46 *Out of the Night*
McVeigh (the Oklahoma Bomber) chose Henley's Invictus as his epitaph and copied it out in his own hand.

About the author

David Anthony lives with his family in Stoke Poges, close to the churchyard where Gray wrote his *Elegy*, a source of much inspiration.
Visitors to the church and Gray's monument can also conveniently view David's bulkhead light, which is fixed above his garage door.